Road Trip

A Personal Journey

Through Life's Detours and Pit Stops

Jessie Seneca

D0109073

A personal journey through life's detours and pit stops

ROAD TRIP

Jessie Seneca

*Ruth
Enjoy the
journey
Love,
Jessie*

Road Trip
A Personal Journey Through Life's Detours and Pit Stops

Copyright © 2013 Jessie Seneca

ISBN 978-1492813668
Religion, Christian Life, Personal Growth

Published by Fruitbearer Publishing, LLC
P.O. Box 777, Georgetown, DE 19947
302.856.6649 • FAX 302.856.7742
www.fruitbearer.com • info@fruitbearer.com

Edited by Connie Rinehold
Proofread by Wilma Caraway
Cover design by Kelly Vanek, Cassidy Communications, Inc.
Interior design by Candy Abbott

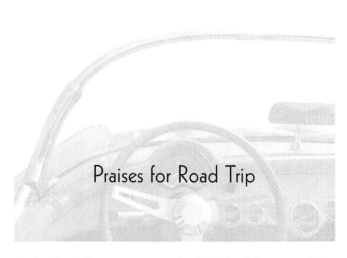

Praises for Road Trip

Author Jessie Seneca compares the Christian life to a road trip with all the potholes, construction detours, traffic jams and challenges one encounters on the road of life. Jessie says, "Your daily ride with God is vital to your daily living." For those who want to grow in Christian character, this book is a must read. Thanks, Jessie, for writing an interesting, entertaining, and captivating book with many valuable lessons for the road trip of life.

~ Pastor Larry Burd
Calvary Baptist Church. Easton, PA

Everyone loves a good story. Jessie takes her life story, adds her personal insights learned along the bumps and curves in the road, and challenges us to live out our stories with the same heavenly perspective. With her gift of reflection and insight, Jessie takes us on a journey which, through her gentle prodding, better equips us to take hold of the Father's hand as we travel down our own road. As someone has said, "What comes from the heart, goes to the heart." Jessie shares her life lessons in such a winsome way that we can't help but gain a more heavenly perspective into our own journeys. Thanks, *Jessie!*

~ Pastor Brian Cooper
Montgomery Evangelical Free Church, NJ

Jessie's story has both captivated me and encouraged me to see my own journey as one He can use. Through this book I'm challenged to trust Him when I'm completely surprised by life's circumstances. Jessie is so brave and gracious to share her journey with us, and I praise God for her transparency. Share this book with someone who needs to be reminded that God never wastes anything!

~ Gayla Mckinney
Pastor's wife, First Baptist Church, Lee's Summit, MO

Road Trip takes you through the twists and turns of Jessie's journey battling Cushing's Syndrome. The power of God moving in her life and others is intertwined throughout her story. God has brought Jessie through her trial victoriously and is now using her experience for His glory. This book will inspire and give hope to anyone going through a life-threatening health issue or a difficult circumstance that seems to have no answers and no end.

~ Susan Scrima
Ministry Assistant, More of Him Ministries, Bethlehem, PA

What a pleasure it was to be along for the ride. *Road Trip* is a remarkably true story of survival, hope, and God's unending grace when life seems like it's veering out of control. Packed with inspiring and road-tested insight from respected speaker, Bible study leader, and author Jessie Seneca. *Road Trip* challenged me to appreciate life's journey and the road ahead.

~ Kelly C. Vanek
Creative Director, Cassidy Communications, Inc., Bethlehem, PA

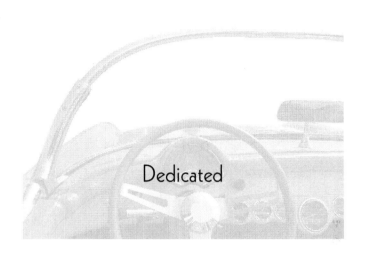

Dedicated

To my sweet daughters
Lauren and Sarah

If it were for your eyes only,
I would have written this:
A mother's legacy
inspired by love for her daughters.

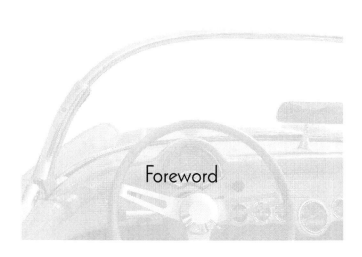

Foreword

Strength. Courage. Patience. Grace. Hope.

These are just a few of the words I would use to describe Jessie Seneca and her journey of faith.

Jessie and I met a number of years ago. At the time, I never dreamed she was a woman who had faced such trials and difficulties in life. She is so vibrant and full of life . . . but sometimes it is those who endure and persist through the storms who finally see the rainbow . . . and point it out to others.

Jessie is one of those people. Jessie's challenges as she struggled through multiple surgeries and illnesses with Cushings was not an easy one. However, through all the bumps and detours, she leaned in and depended more upon God and His great plan for her life.

By the time many of us met Jessie, her character had been tried and strengthened. Much like Daniel, Esther, or other great heroes of the Bible, Jessie stood firm in her conviction and was not one to waver. It is clear that her faith in God and His purposes would override anything she might desire for herself. Her story reflects a life dedicated to God and determined to trust Him above all else.

Road Trip will remind you that your life is an amazing journey full of twists and turns that often bring joy in the most unexpected places. Because no matter where you go in life, regardless of the storms you face . . . Jesus has the power to command the wind and the waves (Mark 4:35-41). He can help you survive and thrive in spite of the storms. That is what He did for Jessie and what He desires to do for you and others who put their faith and trust in Jesus.

I pray you will gain great wisdom and insight into your own journey as you learn from Jessie's experience on her personal road trip.

And Jessie, we are forever grateful to God and His plan that allowed our paths to cross.

$\sim$ Michelle Hicks
LifeWay Women

Table of Contents

Praises for Road Trip v

Dedication vii

Foreword ix

Acknowledgments xiii

How to Use This Book xv

Chapter One   It's Been a Road Trip 17

Chapter Two   God, What About My Plans? 29

Chapter Three   Rearview Mirror 41

Chapter Four   There's a Traffic Jam 51

Chapter Five   Enjoy Your Fellow Travelers 63

Chapter Six   Take Breaks Along the Way 75

Chapter Seven   Capture the Memories 87

Chapter Eight   One Road, Two Views 99

Chapter Nine   Turn Up the Music and Sing Along......109

Chapter Ten   Journey to a Satisfied Life 121

Small Group Discussion Questions 133

About the Author...153

The Secret is Out: Learn it. Live it. Pass it on. 154

Order Info. for Jessie's Books 155

Acknowledgments

As I began writing these words, I realized that, first and foremost, this book is a legacy to you, my daughters Lauren and Sarah. If this book had never made it into the hands of anyone else, I would be fine with that. I want to be absolutely sure that I have shared with you, in every way possible, how much I love God and what He has taught me through the journey of my life. I want to pass that love down to you and to your children, so you may know the deep love of God in your own lives. When it seemed too hard to continue some days, I would look at your smiling faces and push through. As we grew together, your encouragement, love, and even your sarcasm, would make the hours worth the write.

The love and support I have had from both of you girls and your father have been beyond what I ever imagined when I started this journey. I am thankful that you have been the first editors of this book in life and print. We have done this journey together, and I would have never made it through without you by my side. I'll love you forever and like you for always, my sweet girls, sisters in Christ, and best friends. Words can't express all that you both mean to me and how you have inspired me to live a holy life, worthy of His calling, by your examples. I am forever grateful. I love you!

Susan Scrima, if only I could fully express how deeply thankful I am to you for being my dear friend and ministry partner. Without your creative energy and encouragement, this book would have taken a different road. I am forever grateful for your countless hours of first edit, accountability, and love for a good story.

And to my devoted husband, John. You made this possible. You went without lunches, made beds, and invested hours of conversation to allow me to pen the words of our journey together. I love you and thank you for all you have done and do to allow me to follow God's call.

For to me, to live is Christ and to die is gain.
But if I am to live on in the flesh,
this will mean fruitful labor for me . . .
yet to remain on in the flesh
is more necessary for your sake.

Philippians 1:21-24 (NASB)

How to Use This Book

Please use this book in a way that most suits you. You may prefer to read through the book during your alone times with God, those "little beyond" moments in your sanctuary.

If you grow best in a small group with friends, approach this as a five-week book club and complete two chapters each week. Meditate on the "Go Deeper" Scriptures and answer the provided reflective questions at the back of the book. When you come together, discuss the questions and your answers.

Either way you decide to approach this book, I encourage you not to take this journey alone. Invite others to ride with you, pray for you, and spur you on to the beautiful destination God has planned for you.

My prayer is that each of you will begin to view your own journey with God and embrace the traffic jams, the detours, and off-road excursions as the plans God has for you. And along the way, you will take breaks as needed, capture the memories, turn up the music, and sing along.

Enjoy your road trip!

> Trust God from the bottom of your heart;
> don't try to figure out everything on your own.
> Listen for God's voice in everything you do,
> everywhere you go;
> he's the one who will keep you on track.

Proverbs 3:5-6 (MSG)

Chapter One
It's Been a Road Trip

During one of our adventurous trips, my husband, John, and I rented a motorcycle in Arizona and headed for the Grand Canyon. Never having been in that part of the country before, we didn't know what to expect along the way.

We had a sketched map, some clothes to stay a night or two packed in our side-saddlebags, and a journey ahead of us. I had the best view in town—the back seat of the motorcycle, tucked behind the comfort and protection of John.

Yes, the Grand Canyon was spectacular, but it was the adventure of getting there that made the trip worth our while . . .

The towns between Phoenix and our destination.

The small mom and pop coffee shops.

The interesting people we met.

The stories we heard.

The beauty of God's creation.

And yes, even a stop at the local Walmart.

As we traveled upcountry to the Canyon, we were not ready for the drop in temperature. We had to fill up the motorcycle with gas, put on our leather jackets, and buy a pair of gloves to finish out our day of riding.

A few miles outside the entrance to the Canyon, we arrived at a quaint little town just above Flagstaff, where we were thankful for a good Mexican dinner and a good night's rest.

As much as it is good to plan for a trip or an important event that lies ahead, I believe "adjusting" is the most critical part of planning.

Like our trip in Arizona, we had a destination in mind but were soon sidetracked by the events that were not planned.

Rain.

Wind.

Bumpy terrain.

A stop to buy gloves.

> You can make many plans,
> but the Lord's purpose will prevail.
>
> Proverbs 19:21 (NLT)

When the detours of our life surface, that is where "the rubber meets the road." That is where our faith is challenged, our desires questioned, and our trust expanded.

As I look back along the road traveled, I am so grateful that God didn't show me the full map of my life in one viewing. If He had, I am not sure I could have endured.

Instead, He gives me portions of the journey as He reveals His ways through the ride of my life. This is my road trip to share:

In the summer of 1992, I was twenty-seven years old, a young mom of two girls, Lauren—two years old, and Sarah—four months. That summer, we did all the things a stay-at-home mom might do with her children. We went to the community township pool, took walks, and enjoyed the long, lazy days of summer. In our backyard, the girls tried their best to hit the whiffle ball in the grass. And oh, how they anticipated the joy of Daddy walking through the door for our nighttime entertainment.

During these days, although among many fun activities, life began to change. It seemed as though we hit one detour after the next.

Frustrated by the onset of acne on my face, arms, and back. I tried replacing my soaps, shampoos, and detergents, but nothing helped. With the excitement of my favorite season right around the corner, the fall festivities began.

We went on our yearly farm hayride to gather items for our front porch decorations, our traditional pumpkin dinner, and pumpkins for carving.

In my pictures from our harvest adventure, I noticed an apparent physical change in my face. The patches of acne had become worse.

My hands had started to tremble and I was more anxious than usual, but I dismissed that as "normal mom things."

Potty training a two-year-old.

Nursing an infant.

And trying to have dinner on the table on time.

Who wouldn't be a little stressed out?

My puffy face looked as if I'd just had my wisdom teeth removed. With each passing month, things progressed from bad to worse, and I grew more discouraged.

Since I had never been sick before this time and was in the hospital only to have my girls, I really didn't know where to begin. Thankfully, I wasn't sure what was mapped out before me.

The journey began with a trip to our family doctor. He treated me with antidepressants for anxiety.

A home pregnancy test viewed positive, so my next visit was to my gynecologist. Multiple tests showed that I was not pregnant.

I was told the puffiness in my face was the change in bone structure that can develop after childbirth.

Unsatisfied with the outcome of that visit, my frustration continued to build.

Thanksgiving arrived.

I had the entire meal prepared but was unable to serve it due to a very bad anxiety attack.

My sister-in-law was gracious enough to come and retrieve all the food, pick up our girls, and take them to her house for the twenty-plus family members' Thanksgiving dinner.

Feeling as though my world was closing in with little reprieve from the anti-depression medicine, I ended up in the emergency room of a local hospital.

Shortly after that ER visit, feeling as though I could not care properly for my girls with my anxiety hitting it's peak, I made my first trip, with my in-laws coaxing, to the same hospital's psychiatric floor on the day of my brother's birthday. What a present.

I spent that Christmas entrapped in what seemed like a prison to me. I was away from my family . . . in a lonely place . . . unaware of what lay ahead, but very much aware of the dark hours of the present day.

The Doctors determined I had Cushing's Syndrome.

Cushings? I'd never heard of it. What was this? Is it curable? The questions swirled in my head with no escape to be found.

I learned that Cushings is a rare endocrine or hormonal disorder. It occurs when the adrenal glands release too much of the hormone cortisol into your body. Most Cushings tumors are located on the pituitary gland but can present themselves anywhere else in your body, most likely on your lung, adrenal gland, or bronchial tube.

Due to the excess amount of cortisol, many physical and mental problems can occur, which I experienced through the months ahead.

The Christmas hospital stay began a four-month journey at four different facilities, from December through Easter of the following year.

Just a few days after New Year's Eve, I was transported to a city hospital where they performed pituitary surgery to correct the disease. Just days after the surgery, the psychiatric department and the neurosurgeon fought over my release. (Months later, we were informed that this first surgery was unnecessary as there was never a tumor on my pituitary.)

The neurosurgeon won. He felt the surgery was successful and sent me home.

The psychiatrist disagreed due to my unstable state that still remained.

Being home was difficult. Suicidal thoughts increased. John slept on the floor in the foyer by the front door to stop me from exiting the house in the middle of the night.

In less than a week, I had packed my bags for a couple days away, and I was back in a psychiatric facility. Thankfully, this time, it was a Christian center, which became my home for two and a half months. While hospitalized at this facility, my mental state continued to plummet, my physical symptoms continued to become worse, and I was deteriorating at an alarming rate.

Along with the acne, I struggled with increased anxiety, depression, hair growth on my face, a hump at the top of my back, sugar diabetes, loss of bladder control, and thickness around my midriff. Plus, my will to live was gone.

The doctors seemed to be treating only the mental part of the syndrome by putting me on four different tranquilizers, which should never have been mixed with one another.

And then there was a break in the journey. John received a note from a neighbor, who knew a friend of a friend who battled Cushings. She gave him the name of a doctor in Virginia, who had treated her for the same syndrome.

After hearing my story, the doctor's reply was, "You need to bring her down here like, yesterday!"

Leaving behind a difficult discharge from my home-base psychiatric hospital in Pennsylvania, my husband, my brother, and I headed on a five-hour road trip to the University of Virginia Hospital. And a road trip it was!

Once I was admitted, the doctors knew from looking at me what was wrong.

They felt it necessary to do the extensive testing and retesting to confirm their suspicions. The results pointed to an ectopic tumor they found on my left lung and immediately scheduled the surgery to remove the tumor. With John commuting, five-hours away, he wasn't able to make it to the hospital in time to see me off to surgery, but he was by my side as I was wheeled out afterward.

With the removal of the tumor, my cortisol levels drastically dropped to zero, so I needed additional medication for a short time to keep my system in balance.

This surgery was successful, but the thought of being reunited with my family brought waves of emotions I didn't anticipate.

Fear, doubt, and uncertainty became my traveling companions.

Seeing my girls only two times in the last four months caused me to feel less than adequate, and I began to wonder if they would even remember me?

Sarah, who was now close to eleven months old, welcomed me home by walking up to me and saying, "Mama" (she had been coached well, but that is for another story).

Lauren, with her third birthday just around the corner, was excited for mommy to be back home and greeted me with a big hug.

All the reservations I had upon my homecoming were wiped away with a hug and a kiss.

With the passing of each day, things started to become normal.

Three months later, I was back into full swing in motherhood.

Remember when I said earlier that I was glad God hadn't revealed the whole trip to me at once?

The onset of the syndrome, two surgeries, and months away from my family seemed to be more than enough for one person to handle, right?

Yet, there is so much more to the story. Let us fast forward three years to 1995 . . .

When Lauren was entering kindergarten, they found another tumor on the same lung through a routine checkup. I didn't have any symptoms, but it meant another lung surgery.

Even though I was more physically prepared going into this surgery, the haunting memory of all I'd been through seemed to lurk around each corner of my mind, and the thought of what lay ahead was almost more than I could bear.

Thankfully, the recovery was much easier this time around.

In 1999, I started to have similar symptoms. I called my doctors right away. Back to Virginia we headed. The doctors scanned and tested to discover that I had, yes, another tumor on the same lung. This time, we faced either medication by monthly injection or the removal of the rest of my lung.

We went the route of the injection, which worked for three and a half years.

After that time, the medicine ceased to work. The tumor stopped responding, and we were faced with the inevitable: a third thoracic surgery and a full left lung pneumonectomy.

In 2006, we discovered another carcinoid tumor in my chest cavity. It sounded scary because of the location near the aorta, ended up being the easiest of the surgeries. Difficult, yes. But just another detour along the way.

Four hospitals and six surgeries later, I had also been through a tubal ligation and a heart condition to boot.

Since then, I am able to do my day-to-day activities and most things, just at a slower pace. Well, maybe a faster pace than some. I guess it's all relative. Knowing my limitations helped to curb my expectations. But, knowing God's power—now, that increased my productivity.

I feel that God has allowed this in my life to help me stop and enjoy the journey. To savor each day He gives me with appreciation at every turn. To reflect on His goodness. To allow Him to drive. Whenever I try to take the wheel, He puts on the brakes and slows me down to a pace worth living for.

We may have the same goal of reaching heaven, but by the amazing grace of God, we each have a unique way to arrive. We each have our own individual story.

Some a short journey.

Some longer.

Some harder than the next and some easier.

Some with more detours, while others have a smooth journey.

Again, I believe God knows what it is going to take for each one of us to be more like His Son, Jesus Christ. He will do whatever it takes for us to arrive safely in His arms— refining and perfecting our faith along the journey.

Ride "shotgun" with me through my road trip as I discover God around each bend. I hope you enjoy the "God stories," the people you will meet along the way, and a life changed by construction.

Oh, that we would enjoy the journey set before us.

It is no one else's road trip but our own!

Chapter Two
God, What About My Plans?

Until I came upon a major curve in my life, I thought I had it all planned out.

Marriage. Three children—two girls and one boy, in that order.

And a ride into the sunset.

You may be like I was at the onset of my disease—just starting out on your road trip with God, and you think you have it all planned out down to the smallest detail.

You are in the middle of your trip, and you feel as if you are purely in survival mode.

You may be looking back on life's journey with hindsight of each curve and detour along the way with more understanding.

Or upon further review . . .

A little of all three.

You wish you could go back and reset time in some areas of your life, so your days would have taken you on a different path.

Your days are moving faster than you can keep up with. Or, as you look back at all you have learned, you wouldn't trade it for anyone else's ride.

There is a little of the past, present, and future in each of us, yes?

God's plans are your plans; you just may not know or see them, yet.

He has made everything appropriate in its time.
He has also set eternity in their heart,
yet so that man will not find out the work which God has
done from the beginning even to the end.

Ecclesiastes 3:11 (NASB)

Reflect on your personal journey and all that God has revealed to you through the short drives.

Through the long excursions.

Through the busyness.

Through the tranquil.

Some days, we just hop in the car and do what we need to do with little thought until we come upon a detour and then wonder hits us.

Where are they taking me?

How long will it take?

Will I even arrive safely and on time?

These are some of the questions that resonated with me over the years of hospitals, surgeries, and medications. One detour after the next, I wondered, did God have more than just surviving ahead for me? I hope to share "life" with you and what you can learn from your journey through the plans God has for each of you.

And by the end, you will enjoy the ride God has placed before you. You will feel satisfaction, enjoyment, and acceptance. You will realize that God has a call on your life, and He can use all the off road trips for His glory.

Here we go, fasten your seat belts.

> "For I know the plans I have for you,"
> declares the Lord,
> "plans to prosper you and not to harm you,
> plans to give you hope and a future."
>
> Jeremiah 29:11 (NIV)

Growing up in a small town in Pennsylvania was a time and place of safety for me. A place where everyone knew each other and one another's plans. As people would leave on their new life's journey, we would lose touch. But, every now and then, we would be reconnected with excitement or astonishment.

I would often wonder what my journey would resemble.

I had plans . . . Where did they go?

They didn't turn out the way I anticipated.

Or did they? And I just didn't realize it.

Yes, I had it all mapped out in my mind; certainly on paper, it looked good. And maybe, for a while, it was headed in the direction I planned. But then came that sharp curve around an unexpected corner.

O God, You knew. I was headed right for the detour and You knew what was best!

I believe God knows the beginning from the end of your life and all the stops in-between that will make you more like Him.

You may be thinking, life is just plain hard!

Yes, but I am here to tell you, that joy can come to you in and through your struggles. And it may even be better at the backside of that struggle.

So often, we allow the outside circumstances, the detours, along the way to rattle our internal joy that comes from God, don't we?

We shouldn't be surprised when trials come.

But they seem to always catch us off guard, don't they?

What do you do then?

Who do you turn to in time of need?

For you know that when your faith is tested,
your endurance has a chance to grow.
So let it grow,
for when your endurance is fully developed,
you will be perfect and complete,
needing nothing.

James 1:3-4 (NLT)

It is important to turn to your pastor, friends, family or spouse (if married). We certainly need others when the roadblock stops us, but there is no one like the Living God to reach out to.

To hold on to.

To look up to.

Your character will be strengthened as you become more like Christ through your detours.

It is hopeful that:

† You will develop more love for others.

† You will have more joy because you have grown thankful for what He has brought you through.

† Peace will overtake your soul.

† Patience and kindness will be more apparent.

† You will find the good in things and will possess more self-control as you allow the Spirit of God to control your life.

Some of you are in the middle of your detour right now and may be thinking, "What is she talking about?"

Trust me, God always works things for good to those who love Him (see Romans 8:28).

You may not be able to have full view because you are in the middle of a pothole, mucky waters, or side streets; but it will all be clearer after you come through it.

As we read through the Scriptures, we see many people who have struggled:

- † Abraham leaving his home in Ur to go who knew where.
- † Elijah fighting depression.
- † Job losing everything.
- † David running for his life.
- † Naomi feeling abandoned and bitter.
- † Esther approaching possible death in the face of King Xerxes.
- † Joseph thrown into slavery.
- † Paul beaten, ship wrecked, and thrown into jail.
- † Stephen martyred.
- † John abandoned to a remote Island.
- † Jesus Christ crucified.

These are only a few examples. I have felt some of these. Have you experienced:

Rejection?

Abandonment?

Loss?

Despair?

More times than I like to say, I have asked God to remove the thorn in my flesh.

Just as Paul asked three times. I asked three times. But it seemed as though I needed to have the three lung surgeries.

Why?

God, What about my plans?

Hardship and adversity are both a vital part of our walk with God.

If life's journey was always a straight drive from here to there, we would never have the need to look up and view the map of God's Word along the way. We would never experience the wonder of discovery of sudden, irrefutable knowledge.

These detours can either turn you away from God or draw you closer to Him.

I plead with you, don't turn away from Him. Instead, run as fast as you can. No, dash to the foot of the cross.

Second Corinthians 1:8-11 is a Scripture I have drawn on often through my journey. I guess you could call it my life verse:

> We think you ought to know, dear brothers and sisters, about the trouble we went through in the province of Asia. We were crushed and overwhelmed beyond our ability to endure, and we thought we would never live through it.
>
> In fact, we expected to die. But as a result, we stopped relying on ourselves and learned to rely only on God, who raises the dead.
>
> And he did rescue us from mortal danger, and he will rescue us again. We have placed our confidence in him, and he will continue to rescue us.
>
> And you are helping us by praying for us. Then many people will give thanks because God has graciously answered so many prayers for our safety.
>
> 2 Corinthians 1:8-11 (NLT)

Paul felt crushed and overwhelmed almost to the point that he could not endure any longer.

Does that sound familiar to you?

The Greek, rescue or deliver *(rhuomai)* means to draw to oneself.

God may not always remove the obstacle or detours in your life, but it's what He will do for you, in and through the trial.

He will draw you "to Himself" and if you make the Most High your shelter, no evil will conquer you because He orders His angels to protect you (see Psalm 91:10-11).

This is not to say trials won't come, because you know they will, but they will not conquer you if you allow Him to rescue you unto Himself.

> Those who live in the shelter of the Most High
> will find rest in the shadow of the Almighty.
> This I declare about the Lord:
> He alone is my refuge, my place of safety;
> he is my God, and I trust him.
>
> Psalm 91:1-2 (MSG)

For me, it was when I decided to rely on God and not on myself that things began to change.

It was when I allowed God to take the wheel.

It was accepting the road before me that God allowed in my life.

Yes, there were times I wanted to take that steering wheel back. But through the drives and the attempts to allow Him to steer, is where I began to increasingly trust Him.

Have you allowed God to rescue and draw you to Himself?

When you do, you will find comfort and peace there.

He doesn't always take the circumstances out of your journey, and He may not answer your prayers the way you hoped.

But He will always know the best plans for you. Many people can quote Jeremiah 29:11 by heart . . .

"For I know the plans I have for you,"
declares the Lord,
"plans for good and not for evil
to give you a future and a hope."

Jeremiah 29:11 (NIV)

But it is the verses that follow, that we should recall as well.

"Then you will call on me and come and
pray to me, and I will listen to you.
You will seek me and find me when you
seek me with all your heart.
I will be found by you," declares the Lord,
"and will bring you back from captivity."

Jeremiah 29:12-14 (NIV)

There is a part we must play in this journey of life.

Call!

Seek!

Find!

When we seek Him with all our hearts, He will reveal himself to us in ways far greater than we could ever imagine, and He will give us the strength to keep driving.

Journey on, my friend.

Chapter Three

Rearview Mirror

Enthusiasm ran through my mind and heart as I got in my car to drive home after a weekend women's retreat at which I had just been the key speaker. Although I had spoken at many retreats over the years, this one left an indelible mark on me. God had shown me how people responded to my testimony in a fresh way. They seemed to hang onto every word of my story and how God had taken me from the pit to a place of victory by His grace.

As I pulled out from the parking lot, I looked in the rearview mirror and thought, *What a road I have taken to be at this place in my life*, which reminded me of where I had been, where I have traveled, and where I am now.

Let's put our vehicle in reverse for this road trip with a reflection that goes back in time . . .

Jessie with her mom on a road trip down memory lane in 2012, in front of Jessie's childhood home in New Jersey.

I was born to Carl and Kathy Eschenbach, in a small lake community, Kemah Lake, New Jersey in 1965. I was the first grandchild of ten on my mother's side and the only grandbaby girl on my father's side.

My brother, Carl Jr., followed behind me by only seventeen months.

We grew up in a loving, close-knit and supportive family with good memories.

I know after all these years in Women's Ministry that is a rarity, and I thank God for what He protected me from.

Three-year-old Jessie with her dad

Jessie in her early years

In the elementary years of my childhood, my parents moved us to Pennsylvania where they bought the first of three businesses, The Big Star, a corner ice-cream shop, which grew into the "talk of the town." It seemed whatever my parents put their hands to prospered.

The "Big Star," our family business

But even with the busyness of their small town store, they always seemed to keep Carl Jr. and me their top priority. We may have gone without a summer vacation for many years, but we didn't seem to mind. Who would, when you could have a slurpy and the "flavor of the day" ice-cream cone daily?

If we hadn't fallen asleep in the bunk beds they made out of the storage shelves, we were cleaning the countertops for fifty cents a half-hour, which eventually turned into a part-time summer job.

Years and miles won't separate Jessie from her brother.

Whatever they did, my brother and I were never far away.

My dad made me feel like a princess as far back as I can remember. There were times I would get all dressed up and go with him to a restaurant trade show at a classy hotel, and I would feel as if I was the only girl in the room.

Upon entering my tenth-grade year of high school, my parents sold their business to be able to support me and my brother in our athletic pursuits.

They didn't want to miss a second of our competitions. They never missed sitting in the bleachers of a field hockey game, gymnastic meet, or my track events. I knew when the whistle blew, they were there cheering me and my team on.

I met John during my high school years.

I was starting ninth grade, and he, tenth. Little did we know all that God would do through our lives in the years to come.

John and I, both came to a saving knowledge of Jesus Christ after being invited to church by John's mother on a hot summer night in an un-airconditioned city independent church shortly after graduating high school.

He was Catholic.

I was a mix of Presbyterian, Lutheran, and Methodist.

Through my age of seven, my parents were very faithful in taking us to church, but once we moved to Pennsylvania, it became difficult with a thriving business to manage.

I still seemed to find friends who would take me with their families.

I was always drawn to church, enjoyed Sunday school, and even became the president of a youth group. But I didn't fully understand the love of God until that night in 1983 when I felt the pastor was speaking directly to my heart.

Unsure of my future, I trusted it to God and allowed Him to pave the way.

Two years after our conversion, at the age of twenty, I walked the long aisle to John, my high school sweetheart.

Today, we are knocking on the door of thirty years of matrimony and wouldn't trade a moment of all we have learned.

I don't think there is anyone else who would have stuck with me as long as John has.

Like many young couples, we had to figure things out, and there were some areas I wish to be a distant memory. Thanks be to God's grace, they are.

John and Jessie celebrating their 28th anniversary

Five years into our marriage came our first bundle of joy, Lauren Ashley, and then her sister, Sarah Lynne, two years later.

With each addition came the financial struggle of being a stay-at-home mom.

But God always provided for our family in ways far greater than we could ever imagine or hope for.

And here I am all these years later, still a stay-at-home mom going about God's business and forever grateful that John has supported me through this calling.

Raising our girls has been the sweetest part of my life.

Learning much from our own parents about commitment and dedication, inspired us to live that legacy out with our own family. From early on, our girls were faced with my illness—in and out of hospitals, six surgeries, and repeated doctor visits.

Recently, while talking with them about this multiple-decade journey, they shared that they "didn't realize the magnitude of it all as little girls." They seemed to be sheltered by the complexities that came with the distance between our home and the hospitals.

They never saw me when I came out of surgery. They never saw all the tubes, wires, and machines connected to me. They never saw the moments of despair as I fought for my life.

But the effects of recoveries, prayer, church anointing, and moments leading up to each battle have rippled through their lives and made them stronger. While reading their college application essays through tear-filled eyes, I realized the impact this journey of mine has had on them.

I once told a friend, "All I wanted to be able to do was to live long enough to raise my girls."

And now that they are raised and walking closely with the Lord, I still want to live!

I want to see all that God has for them as they approach their young adulthood.

I want to be a part of their future families.

Their highs and their lows.

Their successes and their sorrows.

Each stage is as precious as the last.

As hard as I try to enjoy each phase of my daughters' lives, the moments whiz by so fast, it seems that each becomes a memory before we have finished living it.

Oh, that I would not take for granted the stage of life I am in this very moment.

> For I rejoiced greatly
> when the brothers came and testified to your truth,
> as indeed you are walking in the truth.
>
> 3 John 1:3 (ESV)

Have you heard the saying, "It takes a village to raise a child"?

Well, the king of our village is my faithful husband and our daughters' loving father. John has been the backbone and strong one through everything. He has been a big part of our girls' lives.

They grew close to him through their nightly "setting up camp."

Backyard games.

Family walks.

Little league, travel softball, and yes, he was even their high school coach.

Lauren and Sarah with John—softball days

They have a strong bond with their daddy that reaches as far back to those mornings he would get them ready to meet their sitter while I was hospitalized.

Upon my arrival home from my four-month hospital stay when the girls were just little tykes, I had 24-hour care from friends for weeks while John would go to work.

One of the first mornings, while preparing for the daily arrival of our caretakers, Lauren, then almost three years old, started to throw Cheerios on the kitchen floor. I asked with surprise, "What are you doing, honey?"

"Daddy and I do this every morning!" she responded without missing a beat. They would throw the Cheerios to help occupy Sarah while John packed the car and dressed and prepared Lauren for the day.

Sarah's favorite breakfast?

You guessed it: Cheerios. And a little dirt to boot.

You have to laugh. Even through the difficulties, we managed to find humor in it.

With a man like John by your side, there is no other way to deal with it. He is always keeping us in stitches from laughing so hard.

I love this man!

> A cheerful disposition is good for your health;
> gloom and doom leave you bone-tired.
>
> Proverbs 17:22 (MSG)

It's possible that some readers may think that if they were looking in that rearview mirror, they would make some major adjustments. But sometimes there are things we just can't adjust. We wish we could, but in all reality, we can't.

God's strength will make it possible for us to live above our circumstances.

Learn from your experiences and pass on what you have learned to those who come behind you. In life there is only one thing you can control and adjust.

Your attitude!

Look back, make the necessary adjustments, and drive straight ahead with Godspeed.

Chapter Four

There's a Traffic Jam

Traffic jams just make you want to cringe; don't they? There is nothing like driving along at a steady speed to see those blinking lights a half mile ahead of you.

Just as you have passed a prospective exit ramp and wonder what is happening.

It always seems to be at the worst time and, yes, usually unexpected. What now?

Thankfully, we live in the era of cell phones, GPS, and we can connect with those who will be affected by our tardiness, and, hopefully, find an alternate route.

But at times, there is nowhere to go and nothing we can do to change the situation.

There are certain lessons we wouldn't learn if God didn't stop us.

Make us sit still . . .

And allow ourselves to take in the scenery.

Yes, we may go to great lengths to avoid the evening traffic jam by leaving early.

Staying late at the office.

Taking a short cut.

Or taking the alternate route through town, only to sit with everyone else who had the same idea.

Anything to just avoid sitting.

But does it make sense to take the long way around for the sake of moving?

> I will give you the treasures of darkness
> And hidden wealth of secret places,
> So that you may know that it is I,
> The Lord, the God of Israel,
> who calls you by your name.
>
> Isaiah 45:3 (NASB)

The Lord has no problem allowing a traffic jam in your life if it means you look up and seek Him.

There are great wealth and treasures to be revealed in your darkest hour.

He is positioning you right where He wants you to be.

To receive what He has for you.

And where He wants to take you.

Much of what He has for you includes seeing His glory manifested in a greater capacity than you deem necessary.

Nothing comes as a surprise to God.

He knows what is best for you.

In the stillness, there is much to learn.

Look at some of the benefits you can experience while in the traffic jams of your life:

> Instruction comes *(Numbers 9:8)*
> Justice prevails *(Job 35:14)*
> Patience is learned *(Psalm 37:7)*
> Rescue happens *(Psalm 59:9)*
> Hope arises *(Psalm 62:5)*
> Confidence builds *(Micah 7:7)*
> Rewards given *(Luke 12:37)*
> Promises fulfilled *(Romans 15:4)*
> Valuable harvest redeemed *(James 5:7)*

> And so, dear friends,
> while you are waiting for these things to happen,
> make every effort
> to be found living peaceful lives
> that are pure and blameless in his sight.
>
> 2 Peter 3:14 (NLT)

The most critical part of planning, is adjusting.

And that is what a traffic jam in your life allows.

It allows you to take advantage of the stillness.

To talk and listen to the Lord.

Take hold of the stillness to allow God to open your ears to His voice.

Take advantage of the idle moments already available to you and spend them with God.

Let us consider one of the biggest traffic jams in the word of God, the Israelites journey.

They had no idea what they were in for when they left the captivity of Egypt.

All the hardships that would face them in the wilderness before they entered the Promised Land. To begin with, the ten plagues they had to watch with endurance.

And once the Exodus occurred, God took them the long way around.

Not the direct route.

The jam of the Red Sea.

A road through a barren land—no food or water.

The mountain that stood between God and His people at Sinai.

The breaking down and building up of the tabernacle.

Another jam at the crossing of the Jordan as Joshua stepped into the waters.

Straight to the seven days of marching around Jericho and the conquering of Canaan through the trust of two men who spied out the land and the harlot, Rahab.

I don't want to be too hard on the Israelites because I probably would have found myself grumbling and complaining right along with the others.

Eating the same food day after day.

Wearing the same shoes and clothes year after year.

But God was looking down upon them as a time of testing.

Remember how the Lord your God
led you all the way in the wilderness these forty years,
to humble and test you
in order to know what was in your heart,
whether or not you would keep his commands.

Deuteronomy 8:2 (NIV)

I am sure the Israelites were glad, looking back, that God didn't show them their entire journey of forty years and beyond. They might have decided not to leave Egypt.

It is when we look back over our lives that we glean the valuable lessons of darkness.

Just as we are glad that our lives are not mapped out before us, He teaches us as we go through the trials He allows.

I wouldn't want it any other way.

There is hope on this side of the jam and promise on the other.

Every hardship I faced, I faced with Him at my side. And through each one, He taught me something new.

Which brought me closer to Him and helped mold me to be more like His son, Jesus Christ.

It built my character.

Taught me to persevere.

It made me the person I am today.

I am not perfect.

But, oh, I am so much better.

Even with all my faults, He still uses me as long as I am willing to be used for His glory.

Learn the path He has shown you. Always be aware of what He is teaching you and be the best learner you can be through the difficulty.

Look at the trials He allows in your life as a new route to the next level of faith in your journey.

The more trials you come through, the more miles your faith will take you.

It will make it easier to face the next trial.

To keep from getting lost.

Please don't misunderstand me, it isn't always easy. I often thought to myself, *God, What about my plans?*

But, what we have to understand is that God really does care about everything we go through.

He cares about your desires.

He cares about your dreams.

It is just that His ways are better for you and He knows that, though you may not understand it at the time.

He knows and sees the bigger picture.

He is mapping out your life together with the lives of others—some who believe in Him and some who don't.

It may look beautiful at your destination.

And if you were to look back at the road you just traveled, you would see many obstacles that wouldn't look so appealing.

It is the potholes and construction detours that cause you to grow and allow you to shine for Him.

It is what makes you more radiant at the entrance to glory.

He will always be working on the highways until He calls you home to be with Him.

While my girls were in middle and high school, we learned a tough life lesson that was difficult for all of us.

We hit a major traffic jam in the lives of our teenagers when a trip we had planned for over a year took another route.

For many months, I had heart palpitations.

The fear of what may lie ahead and the busyness of life kept me away from the doctor until a visit to my father's hospital bedside. He was battling an aneurysm in his aorta, and seeing him helpless brought me to my knees.

It was there that I knew I needed to see a cardiologist.

My emergency visit with the doctor was on a Friday, and that Sunday we were to leave for Hawaii with another family.

After my visit, the doctor said that he needed to do further testing and a heart catheterization.

Which meant that he didn't want me to make that long flight from the East Coast to the Island of Maui.

But we had planned for over a year for this trip. The spare room had clothes scattered and suitcases packed for months before our departure date.

What does one do, but say, "God what about my plans?"

I was not only able to learn a valuable lesson myself but to teach our girls that sometimes life doesn't go the way we think it should go. Life simply, at times, is just not fair.

It is hard for any of us, but especially for thirteen- and fifteen-year old girls, ready for the trip of a lifetime, when expectations beyond their wildest dreams are cut short by yet another family crisis.

They were supposed to be . . .

Sunbathing.

Snorkeling.

Whale watching.

And it was all going to happen without them.

Instead, they were just thinking about their friends vacationing in Hawaii. What are they going to tell their classmates when they returned to school on Monday morning?

Yes, I made them go to school.

This many years later, they still wish for the opportunity they missed.

But I tell them, "There is always your honeymoon."

Some things are worth the wait.

> I know, God, that mere mortals
> can't run their own lives,
> That men and women
> don't have what it takes to take charge of life.
>
> Jeremiah 10:23 (MSG)

What is most important when our plans don't work out the way we think they should?

It is our attitude and our response to the trials that come into our lives.

You may, for a time, become weary and self-focused, but you must not stay there.

You have to take your eyes off your circumstances and look up.

You must acknowledge what God has allowed in your life, then accept it.

And, finally, adjust your life to the outcome.

Are you going to have a wilderness attitude?

One of complaining and inconvenience?

Or a Promised Land attitude?

One of gratitude and abundance?

If you fail to adjust, you will not be able to be used fully by Him.

God wants you to live for Him and be used by Him.

These trials happen for our "soul purpose"—for the benefit of our mind, will, and emotions.

They happen that we may help others along in their faith journey as well.

People are watching your actions and reactions to the obstacles you hit.

The way you respond will show where (or Who) you are getting your strength from.

Show your spiritual maturity.

It will give you an opportunity to share the love of God with others.

You can only live strengthened lives because you are hidden in Christ with God.

Why hidden?

The intimacy that exists between Christ and His people is hidden from the eyes of the men and women of this world.

Those who walk in the flesh, not by faith, see us going about our daily tasks unaware that our strength by which we live and move and have our being is drawn from God.

That is why it is so important to reach up to God daily for our strength.

So we will be able to act justly, love mercy, and walk humbly with our God.

What others see is the tip of the iceberg.

They don't see what lies beneath the water line, because we are hidden in Christ. It is the power of Christ in you, the hope of glory (Col. 1:27) that will empower you. It is His passion within you that allows you to press beyond your own abilities.

You can find strength down deep where others don't see.

Your daily ride with God is vital to your daily living.

Below the water line is where important stuff happens with God.

Below the water line is where you discover all the treasures of wisdom and knowledge that are hidden in Jesus Christ (Col. 2:3).

And this is why when others see you, the tip of the iceberg, they see strength, power, and perseverance.

Are you able to praise Him in the good times as well as the tough times?

A friend once said to me, "It is the 'test' part of testimony that makes our testimony."

So simple, but so profound.

My life is an example to many
because God is my strength and protection.
That is why I can never stop praising you;
I declare your glory all day long.

Psalm 71:7-8 (NLT)

Chapter Five
Enjoy Your Fellow Travelers

Preparing for a trip is just part of the journey.

Once everything is ready to go.

Packed and placed in its rightful place.

You just need those who are accompanying you to join in. What good is a road trip if you don't share the adventure?

Yes, sometimes we need the alone trips, but it is always more fun with family and friends.

Part of our family trips are the journeys—the rides to our planned place of destination. Our family joke is, "What is said and done in the car, stays in the car."

When we take fellow travelers with us, they have been known to say that our trips should be a reality show.

I am not sure if we should take that as a compliment or not, but our trips are definitely memorable and fun.

During our summer vacation to Smith Mountain Lake in Virginia, about a six-hour trip, we were able to bring our two golden-doodles, Bella and Murphy. I believe our dogs love the trip and the lake more than we do.

As we drove just a few miles away from home, they were not satisfied with being in the back of our SUV.

They quickly jumped over the seats to the second row and inched their way in between the bucket seats in the front.

After some shifting around and our first pit stop, I soon wound up in the back of the truck with, yes, both dogs.

The luggage.

The coolers.

And a good book.

It may have been slightly crowded, but I was still able to enjoy both the conversation and the love from my canine friends.

Murphy and Jessie enjoying their travels

Returning home, I started out in the back with a little more room planned.

It's not always the comfort of the journey we enjoy, but it is those who go with us who make the trip worthwhile.

Part of enjoying our fellow travelers is receiving from them.

Do you find it easier to receive love and help from others, or are you better at giving the help and love?

I am not as good at receiving love as I am giving it.

This is an area that God has needed to teach me and teach me he did.

Now it was up to me to put it into practice.

I found, when I didn't receive from others and enjoy the help and care given, it was flat out, Pride.

Pride leads to disgrace, but with humility comes wisdom (see Proverbs 11:2).

I know it is hard to humble oureselves, but that is what it takes to receive what God wants to give us.

When you and I don't receive from others, we are not allowing them to enjoy their blessings—the blessing God intended for them and the privilege of being a part of your life and mine.

Your family and friends love to help.

Allow them to use their gifts.

When I was first sick, oh, how often I asked others to pray for me.

Only to discover they already were.

My longest and strongest prayers uttered were, "Jesus, I love You."

Believe me, I could not have gotten through this dark period in my life without others praying.

Because I was so unstable and mentally deteriorating, I was finding it difficult to receive the prayers.

At that point, I had the faith only of a mustard seed.

But God's word reminds us that small amount of faith is all we need to move the mountains in front of us.

I can remember my Christian counselors in the psychiatric hospital praying over me as I lay in my bed.

They prayed such sweet prayers, and they assured me that God hears the prayers of his saints and responds in ways we can never imagine.

Approaching my second lung surgery, I again asked for prayers.

I was more coherent at this time, but I just didn't grasp how wide and deep God's love was for me.

You would think I would have gotten it by then.

God knew it would take the third lung surgery for it to fully sink in.

Knowing that God is right in the middle of what is going on in your life and that all things are filtered through his finger became so much a reality to me that it was hard for me to keep quiet about what He was doing.

If you look up Exodus 17:8-16, you will see Moses sending Joshua and the Israelites into battle and standing on the top of the mountain with Hur and Aaron.

Every time Moses became tired, his arms would fall down.

The Israelites would start losing the battle, but when Aaron and Hur came alongside of Moses and held up his arms, Israel started to win.

This is like us, today.

We have to allow others to come alongside of us and uphold us in prayer and sometimes physically come alongside of us to keep our hands on the wheel.

When you allow others to cook your meals.

Help take care of carpooling.

Pick up your groceries.

Wash your clothes.

Or whatever you or your family may need done.

That is the body of Christ working together.

Two people are better off than one,
for they can help each other succeed.
If one person falls,
the other can reach out and help.
But someone who falls alone is in real trouble.

> Likewise, two people lying close together
> can keep each other warm.
> But how can one be warm alone?
> A person standing alone can be attacked and defeated,
> but two can stand back-to-back and conquer.
> Three are even better,
> for a triple-braided cord is not easily broken.

Ecclesiastes 4:9-12 (NLT)

You can have the full body of armor on and stand firm.

With the belt of truth buckled around your waist.

The breastplate of righteousness in place.

Your feet fitted with the readiness that comes from the gospel of peace.

You can take up the shield of faith, with which you can extinguish all the flaming arrows of the evil one.

You can put on the helmet of salvation.

Have the sword of the Spirit, which is the word of God.

And with all this, you can still have your backside uncovered (see Ephesians 6:10-18).

As you read Ecclesiastes 4:9-12, you will see if two believers come together with the full armor of God on and stand back to back, they can conquer.

They will be completely covered on all sides, even their backs.

So, you must allow others to join you.

Uphold you.

Enjoy your fellow travelers.

Without them, you will not only fall, but you will become extremely lonely.

You certainly need to have your closest friends and family come alongside.

At times, you may need to come before God in a corporate setting.

It may mean coming before your local church to have your pastor anoint you with oil.

By doing this, you will be able to share what God is teaching you through your trials.

You allow others a glimpse of what is happening in your life.

A willingness to be vulnerable by articulating your need guides them to know how to pray specifically for you.

It encourages them in their own faith.

And helps them to grow.

It brings those who may not have a prayer life into a more intimate one.

The way you handle your trial may well help others draw closer to Jesus Christ.

It's not for you to keep to yourself but to share with the body of believers.

Having others pray for you will send you away uplifted and ready to face a difficult situation. Won't you allow others to share in the blessing of traveling with you?

As you travel through your life, you will have some memorable travelers who journey with you.

You may have received cards from some that may be tucked away, and you occasionally pull them out for encouragement.

A gift you received from that special person, that as you gaze upon it, you smile with special remembrance of them.

Or, there are moments that are embedded in your mind forever that build your faith.

Then there are some people who just don't have anything tangible to show for their passage except their very own life's example.

I want you to meet some of my fellow travelers:

John, whom you have already met.

John is my very best friend as well as my husband. Together, we have been through some difficult times, but he was always by my side and never left me alone. He trudged through the blizzards of 1992 and '93 for hospital visits, took care of the girls, home, and work. With each detour, he was always there; with each bend, he cared for me; with every bump, he held me up. Through our journey, we have grown closer and count on one another to cheer each other on.

My parents.

They were unable to be by my side daily because of the miles that separated us, but they kept a watchful eye and were able to be with me for the major surgeries. Knowing the care of a mother and father brings comfort, even when it is by prayer and supplication. This love is not always physically seen, but unconditional and forever present.

John's parents.

Their countless hours of moving into our home to care for the girls through many of my surgeries. They were a ray of brightness in a fogged cloud. They kept the routine of their days going and bonds were forged that will last a lifetime.

During my four-month hospital stay, I had many friends and family who pitched in to help John. I would like to share with you about one in particular.

A dear friend, Sarah.

She sacrificed herself and her own daily life for mine. She brought everything she was involved with to a screeching halt to take care of our two girls, a toddler and infant, four days a week, so John would not have to put them into daycare. She cared for my girls as if they were her own along with her elementary-age boys. Months later, after I recovered, I asked her why and how she did it. She responded, "I was doing it unto God, and the Holy Spirit gave me the strength I needed every day." The effect of this sacrificial act of kindness went far beyond our immediate family. It also touched the lives of all who knew her, and it is still touching those who hear about her self-sacrificing love for a friend.

She was the greatest example of friendship to me.

A loving church and neighborhood family.

Without them, we would not have survived. Between the two, my family was provided meals—the church alternated with the neighbors, every two weeks, for the four months and beyond. Our family is why our churches have gone to disposable dishes when preparing meals for families. Seriously, these God-given friends are the backbone of our survival. One neighborhood woman went beyond the call when she extended her hand to us by sharing the story of a friend who had Cushings. That friend, whom we never met, was responsible for us being able to reach our destination at the University of Virginia Hospital. Some friends are for a moment, they come and go, but they are like an angel sent by God to protect and care for us.

I owe a debt of gratitude to Doris, my hair stylist, and Bert, my pastor's wife, as well as Lori, with her soothing guitar, and Melanie, who always has a caring word.

Against my will and John's request, these four dear friends visited me in the psychiatric hospital and attempted through their visits to beautify me with a trim, a hug, and soothing music. It may not have done much for my current state, but the effects of their kindness reached beyond that day to friendships that will last for eternity. It showed me that it is good to act on what God asks of you even when it doesn't make sense.

Our daughters, Lauren and Sarah.

Lauren was only two and a half years old when I was first hospitalized, but even then, she understood nurturing. She nursed her daddy back to health through strep-throat and watched over her baby sister. As the girls grew, my battles continued through multiple surgeries and recoveries. As they watched from a distance without full understanding, God was working in and through both of them to build their faith. Thankfully, today we are on the other side of this journey. My desire and prayers were always to be able to raise my girls to adulthood. God was so gracious to extend my days so I would be able to teach them the admonition of the Lord. Today, we are the best of friends and we never take life for granted. I always tell them to enjoy this day the Lord has given you, it is a gift.

Recently, while reading in 1 Thessalonians 4:9-10, where Paul confirms the Thessalonians' love for their brothers, he encourages them to excel still more.

But we don't need to write to you
about the importance of loving each other,
for God himself has taught you to love one another.
Indeed, you already show your love
for all the believers throughout Macedonia.
Even so, dear brothers and sisters,
we urge you to love them even more.

1 Thessalonians 4:9-10 (NLT)

I was so moved by this Scripture as it convicted me to love as my fellow travelers had loved me over these years.

They are examples I want to emulate.

I want to excel still more.

You can never out-give your love and care for those who journey with you.

Chapter Six

Take Breaks Along the Way

Do you, at times, feel that you are speeding through your days?

Your journey is going at a pace you cannot catch up with?

Those days shortly turn into months, and at the end of another year, you look back and wonder where it all went?

Your life seems to be on the fast track, and you can't stop it!

In this chapter, I want us to stop for a few moments.

Continue with caution.

And move on with courage and strength.

If you allow margin in your life, you will be able to hit some red lights along the way.

I know when I have kept margin in my life, I have allowed God to fill my days with what He wants to see accomplished.

Please don't sit there and think I have figured this one out.

I am just like you, battling the Hurried-Woman Syndrome in the twenty-first century.

Because we live in a fast-paced society, we are going to have to be deliberate about scheduling breaks along the way.

Sometimes, God will schedule them for us without asking our opinion.

When He has done this in my life, He always knew what was best and what it was going to take to get my attention, even if it was from a hospital bed.

I remember going into my second lung surgery with much wonder and fear of a repeat experience as the first.

Would it be the same?

Would it be as difficult?

Would I live through it?

What do You want to teach me, God?

So many questions that may not have been answered the way I hoped.

Soon after I came out of ICU, I was placed in a room with an elderly woman, who had only been in the hospital once before, to give birth to her child.

As we both lay on our beds battling pain with tear-filled eyes, we were unable to see one another through the pulled curtain between our beds.

This elderly woman cried out with terror and panic. The nurses tried to comfort her but to no avail. After the nurses left our room, her whimpering continued, and I wondered, *What can I do for her?*

I was in as bad a shape as my neighbor.

I felt God say to me, *Sing to her.*

"What?"

Sing to her?

God, don't you remember, I only sing in the shower and while driving by myself. Are you sure about this one?

Sing to her, the pressing small voice continued.

Being obedient, I began to sing "Amazing Grace" to her through our drawn barrier.

Believe me, when I say this was a "God thing," it was a "God thing."

Faintly from the other side, with her crackling voice, I heard her say, "Thank you!"

I quickly saw God's plan unfold before my eyes.

I now knew why I was going through what God allowed.

It wasn't about me, but about a woman I would never come across again.

No, it wasn't what I planned.

But remember God's plans are your plans; you just may not know or see them, yet.

> The steps of a man
> are established by the Lord,
> And He delights in his ways.
>
> Psalm 37:23 (NASB)

You may have breaks that God's hand forcibly has for you and you couldn't understand it until you were right smack dab in the middle of His will, similar to the story I shared.

But there are other breaks that we can certainly tend to, breaks that we can create.

Today, words and phrases like:

Take a break.

Wait.

Wait patiently.

Catch your breath.

Be still.

Be quiet . . . are not even part of our vocabulary.

Young moms, working women, stay-at-home moms and grandmothers all have this in common, words and phrases like:

Multitask.

Hurry up.

Let's go.

We're going to be late.

No time to be still is more likely what we are accustomed to in our day.

From the book, *Having a Mary Heart in a Martha World* by Joanna Weaver: "While the world applauds achievement, God desires companionship."

The world clamors, "Do more. Be all you can be!"

Our Father whispers, "Be still and know that I am God."

Let's take a break from the frenzy of our day and take a moment and see what God's word desires for us:

Wait for the LORD;
be strong and take heart and wait for the LORD.
Psalm 27:14 (NIV)

Be still in the presence of the Lord,
and wait patiently for him to act.

Psalm 37:7a (NLT)

"Be still, and know that I am God;
I will be exalted among the nations,
I will be exalted in the earth."

Psalm 46:10 (NIV)

God, my shepherd! I don't need a thing.
You have bedded me down in lush meadows,
you find me quiet pools to drink from.
True to your word,
you let me catch my breath
and send me in the right direction.

Psalm 23:1-3 (MSG)

I wait quietly before God,

for my victory comes from him.

Psalm 62:1 (NLT)

Then I went into your sanctuary, O God.

Psalm 73:17 (NLT)

Instead, I have calmed and quieted myself,

like a weaned child

who no longer cries for its mother's milk.

Yes, like a weaned child is my soul within me.

Psalm 131:2 (NLT)

The Lord is good to those who wait for Him,

To the person who seeks Him.

Lamentations 3:25 (NASB)

Do you take the much needed break throughout your day to be with God?

In Psalm 73:17, Asaph found where he needed to go to connect with God. His sanctuary was where he would hear from God.

The meaning of sanctuary is a consecrated thing or place. A holy place.

A hallowed part.

A cleansing river.

Do you have a place that you call your sanctuary?

Oh, you may walk by that sanctuary place every day and say, I once met with God there, but because of busyness, I just can't find my way back.

It may have been or still is a wrought-iron chair by a babbling brook.

A comfy family room couch.

The end of your dining room table.

Your commute to and from work.

Wherever it is for you, have you taken the time needed for rejuvenation?

Eliminating hurry can make us feel unproductive.

But what if times that seem "unproductive" actually aren't?

I mean times when you focus simply on being with God.

Slowing down is a process.

Taking one step at a time is the only way to engage in this process.

If you have not been able to meet with God for some time, today is a new day. Start over.

Return to Him and live.

Never feel guilty for the time you spend with your heavenly Father.

You become whoever you spend the most time with.

If you have learned that and can't make it through your day without this time and place with Him, you are on the right path.

Let your eyes look directly ahead
And let your gaze be fixed straight in front of you.
Watch the path of your feet
And all your ways will be established.
Do not turn to the right nor to your left;
Turn your foot from evil.

Proverbs 4:25-27 (NASB)

Before my third lung surgery, my sanctuary, where I met with God daily, was at the end of my dining room table.

On this one particular day, I happened to be studying Psalm 91 and how the wings of God protect us.

The power of His presence was so strong that I felt as though I was encamped in His arms.

Deep in His bosom.

An umbrella of shelter was over me.

It was a place I didn't want to leave.

But life called, and I knew I needed to go about my daily tasks.

It was there that I felt God speak into the depths of my soul and give me power to handle the road set before me.

Is it always easy?

No!

But under His wings.

There is power.

There is strength.

There is joy.

Peace and hope.

The same wings that protect you are the same wings that you can soar upon through your hardest moments.

Darkest hours.

And daunting situations.

Under His wings, you safely abide.
Though the night deepens and tempest are wild;
still you can trust him,
to know He will keep you.
He has redeemed you and you are His child.

~ William Cushing ~

Through the breaks God orchestrates along our journey, we should look at them through eyes of wonder.

Eyes of insight and eyes of obedience.

God wants to teach us new lessons about Himself.

His character.

His love.

Our desire should be that we set out to be the best learners we can be through our detours, breaks, stops, and destinations.

> Let me hear Your lovingkindness in the morning;
> For I trust in You;
> Teach me the way in which I should walk;
> For to You I lift up my soul.
>
> Psalm 143:8 (NASB)

It has been through the detours and the breaks along the journey where I have learned the most from God.

He has taught me: patience, trust, obedience, joy, and so much more.

If everything were always "good," we would have no reason to look up and allow God to rescue us and pull us out of the net (Psalm 25:15).

Learning to wait on God, can be hard.

When you feel the pull to move ahead, especially when you felt Him call you into a particular mission or vision in your life and you are not seeing the fruit of that call yet.

Trust!

It may have been ten years.

Fifteen years.

Or, even twenty-plus years ago when you heard His voice and were certain of it.

And you wonder, *why it isn't happening* in a particular time?

He may be saying to you, *Wait!*

I have had this happen multiple times over my life with a period of fourteen years before He brought to fruition what He called me to do and to become.

Was the wait hard? You bet! Was it worth the wait? Absolutely!

Let me share with you the writing of this book.

As I drove away from a retreat in the spring of 2013, during the three-hour drive homeward bound, I reminisced with the Lord about the weekend, the newfound friends I met, and the memories made. After thinking back on the session where I shared my testimony, I felt the Lord speak into my heart, *Your book*.

My book, I thought? I haven't worked on that for eight years. So, the next week after arriving home, I pulled up the book on my computer and started to write, add to, take away from. And there I was, four weeks later, with six chapters written.

Since the writing of my first Bible study, *The Secret is Out,* a study from the book of Colossians in 2010, I had wanted to begin to write another study. I had plans to begin writing my next Bible study in the fall of 2012, but I felt God say, *Wait.* I didn't understand why I was to wait, but I have walked with

God for three decades, and one of the things I have learned, is to listen to Him and to obey Him. When I do that, peace always follows.

As the year continued, I stayed obedient to the waiting. Yes, I was still doing things for God as opportunities arose, but in this particular area of writing, I waited and waited and waited. The wait seemed to be long, but in reality, the timing was perfect and God knew it!

If I had started to write the Bible study when I planned and didn't wait on God, I am not sure I would have heard His voice to pick up this book I began many years ago.

It was in the waiting, I listened.

His timing is perfect.

Don't step before Him.

Allow Him to go before you.

Continue with caution.

And move on with courage and strength.

Chapter Seven
Capture the Memories

I have a drawer filled with many photos from years gone by. A few creative memory albums under the coffee table.

Plenty of the old fashion style albums, you know, the ones you slide the pictures into a sleeve and write the memory next to the photo.

Unprinted photos on my computer and smart phone.

Both our girls are young adult women now.

But still, upon their arrival home with their boyfriends, schoolmates, and friends, they seem to congregate around the picture albums and sometimes even the home videos.

As our girls were growing up, I wanted to try to capture the important stages of their lives by keeping a special box with their accomplishments.

Certificates.

Written letters.

Drawn pictures.

Paper maché animals.

And so much more.

When reopening the over-stuffed boxes, we laugh and remember.

The whens.

The what ifs.

The joys.

Recently, John's dad had some of their family's old videos converted to DVD format.

We have had so much fun at our gatherings watching the aunts and uncles in their prime of high school and younger years.

Watching all our nieces and nephews laughing and seeing their parents resemblances to themselves brings smiles to our hearts.

We are so thankful that Dad captured those precious moments.

And the next generation is, well, I guess you can say, blessed.

Sometimes there are blushed faces but, for the most part, pure laughter and joy.

There are many different ways we can relive our lives, which are vital in remembering the memories.

Some will bring a tear to your eyes.

Others, laughter.

Hopefully, each memory captured will point us to delight in seeing where we once were and from where we have come.

They may have their own style, but they all have the same purpose, making memories.

As I grow older, I try so hard to keep the memories alive. But as hard as I try, there are ones that slip by me.

I have even looked at a picture of one of our girls when they were small and wonder, *Which girl is that?*

I never thought I could forget, but I did. Some memories, we wish we could forget, don't we?

But all your memories are part of who you are and what you are becoming.

The enjoyable memories are so much easier to reflect on.

The difficult memories are the ones where I have learned the most about myself and the Sovereignty of God.

While in the second psychiatric hospital, for two and a half months, there were plenty of memories I wish not to remember.

I can't say that I did.

Even though I was in a precarious state, I remember everything that happened to me.

The thought of the dreaded "rubber room" where I saw a person put in a straight jacket and taken away.

Eating every meal at the nurses' station.

Being weighed backwards because they said I was becoming anorexic.

But what do you expect when you are put on a 1200 calorie diet due to sugar diabetes.

And the most fattening thing you eat is Jell-O.

Laying on the same bed for days, only to watch the clock tick the hours away.

The daily visit from the psychiatrist and the conversation always the same.

"How do you feel today, Jessie?"

"I feel like killing myself."

These are not words you want to quote or relive, but that was what the memory tape kept playing as I hit rewind.

However, I was very thankful for the wonderful Christian counselors who sat by my bedside day in and day out.

Their prayers.

Their encouragement that one day I would be sharing this experience with other women. Even though, I couldn't see a way through the existing day.

They were able to help overshadow the dark cloud that seemed to follow me around every turn.

During my illness, it was hard to comprehend God's will in it and believe the prayers of these women who were only in my life for a short season.

And then, I can vividly recall the day John walked into my cold, sterile room and said, "We are leaving for another hospital."

It was the day the lunch tray became too heavy for me to carry, and I fell in the hall as I was trying to put it away.

As much as I wanted this dark place to become a fading memory, it felt like home.

It seemed to be all that I knew.

Trusting John, but unsure of the destination, I followed.

Little did I know all that transpired to change the course of our direction until months later when I would hear John retell his story.

The memory of a cold winter night when our neighbor brought John that piece of paper, with her friend's contact information on it, shows me the hand of God on our lives. You see, after receiving the information, John threw the paper in the garbage. He was exhausted from the daily grind, and he knew I had been accepted to another hospital, even though it would take close to another eight weeks for admission. In the middle of that night, he was prompted to go dig that stained piece of paper out of the garbage. The next morning, he called the woman, whom God would use to redirect our path to the University of Virginia Hospital.

Shortly before we left for Virginia, my father flew in from Florida where he and my mother owned and operated a restaurant.

At the time, my dad thought he would be able to sweep in like a knight in shining armor and fix everything.

Soon after arriving, he realized the situation was bigger than a daddy rescuing his little girl. It was going to take a miracle of God. Upon much persuasion and against my will, he captured the only photo taken during the full four months of my hospitalization. This was not a photo I wanted taken at the moment, but this many years later, I am so grateful for a father's love.

While hospitalized with
Cushing's Syndrome
February 1993

Three months after
first lung surgery
July 1993

With pictures in mind, the nurses at the University of Virginia would constantly view the photos John placed on the table top in my hospital room. With amazement, but not shock, they would assure me that I would get better and look like the young woman in those pictures again.

I could hardly believe their words. It seemed that I would remain in this state forever.

Yet, they had relived this scene many times before. I was like the countless patients who came through their doors from all over the country with a similar diagnosis.

I revisited the floor for my three-month check-up in the summer of 1993, and the nurses who had so lovingly cared for me said, "You look like a princess."

They had seen me at my ugliest, not just in looks but in attitude.

And they could see beyond all the meanness that changed my personality.

It is memories like this that are embedded in my heart, mind, and soul rather than on paper.

And then there is the snapshot of my parents' faces.

On a sunny fall afternoon in 2002, John and I met my parents, who arrived from Florida, and my brother, who drove in from New Jersey.

We met at a restaurant near the University of Virginia Hospital.

I was preparing for my third lung surgery and full removal of it.

During our dinner hour, I was able to share with my family how God was working in my life.

All that He was teaching me.

All the special moments I captured with God along the way.

Ones I would never have learned without this time.

A time we thought was a hardship, but in all reality was just what the Doctor prescribed.

The looks on my parents' faces were of pride and amazement.

After being wheeled into ICU following the surgery, it seemed as though it was another successful surgery.

Once my brother saw I was stabilized, he needed to make the long drive back to his family.

But soon after he left, things started to take a turn for the worse. With each attempt of the necessary chest x-ray, I was unable to sit up.

As my blood pressure would continually plummet with every vertical movement.

With only John and the nurses in the room with me, John feeding me ice chips, and the nurses keeping me comfortable by laying me horizontal on the bed.

Which seemed as if I was standing on my head.

The infusions of blood and plasma helped, but not enough.

Unbeknown to me, John left the hospital with the prodding of the nurses.

He was settled back in his hotel room, trying to start a movie on his laptop to drown out the memories of the day, when a thought crossed his mind. He said he wasn't sure where that thought came from—it must have been from God.

Obedient to the prompting of the Holy Spirit, he called the nurses' station in the early hours of the morning and asked if the doctors had given me cortisol before my surgery.

No sound resonated from the other end of the phone.

Within moments, my doctor had given the order, and the nurse appeard at my bedside with an injection of cortisol.

I would need this injection before each surgery to help with the recovery as each time a tumor would be removed my cortisol levels would drastically lower.

Without cortisol in your body you are unable to live.

Once this was given, I felt like I could do cartwheels and life came back into these dry bones.

We learned firsthand how the obedience to God's voice, when followed, brings great joy, and we were thankful once again to John's willingness to listen, obey, and act on that still small voice.

How one small correction can make the difference in an outcome.

May I be honest with you? Even though some of the memories are ones I wished for another time or not at all, they became life lessons that could only be captured in the secret places with God.

They were memories learned through the darkness that became beacons of light for my next step.

Moments of despair that became building blocks for developed strength.

Loss of days that brought appreciation for the here and now.

And off-road trips that always brought me back to the hope of my future.

> "I will give you the treasures of darkness
> And hidden wealth of secret places,
> So that you may know that it is I,
> The LORD, the God of Israel,
> who calls you by your name."
>
> Isaiah 45:3 (NASB)

Then there are memories that are only captured through our mind's eye.

Some of them can be captured with a photo.

But these memories are more preciously stored in the memory boxes of our intellect.

As the years flash in front of me with roads of bumpy terrain, some of the captured memories are the twinkling eyes of a baby as I sat in solitude.

A toddler's smile while swinging.

A kindergartner's packed lunch box.

A play date with friends at the community park.

The joys of a sticker received from a memorized Bible verse.

A middle-schoolers first dance.

A high-schooler's search for independence.

A college student's source of accomplishment and dreams of the future.

A written letter from my daughter, also my friend.

These are milestone moments, ones that will never be repeated but forever implanted into my psyche.

Even though some of our photos are hard to look at and you may not want to recapture specific events, it is always good to have that rearview mirror glimpse.

Capture moments along the way to remember the road you have traveled and all that God has brought you through to appreciate the present journey of life.

They will be teachable moments, not for yourself only, but for those of which you want to impart memories of God's grace and love.

Chapter Eight

One Road, Two Views

Hindsight is always 20/20. Well, at least, for me it has been.

As I look back over my life, it seems that it is coming into fuller view with each passing year.

When I consider the road that lies ahead of me and the road I have taken to bring me to this point, I begin to understand God's view compared to my view.

I start to see His plan unfold before me.

The poem that comes to my mind is the one that is cross-stitched, framed, and hanging in my spare bedroom.

Footprints in the Sand
by Margaret Fishback Powers

One night I dreamed a dream.
As I was walking along the beach with my Lord.
Across the dark sky flashed scenes from my life.

For each scene, I noticed two sets of footprints in the sand,
One belonging to me and one to my Lord.
After the last scene of my life flashed before me,
I looked back at the footprints in the sand.
I noticed that at many times along the path of my life,
especially at the very lowest and saddest times,
there was only one set of footprints.
This really troubled me,
so I asked the Lord about it.
"Lord, you said once I decided to follow you,
You'd walk with me all the way.
But I noticed that during the saddest
and most troublesome times of my life,
there was only one set of footprints.
I don't understand why,
when I needed You the most, you would leave me."
He whispered,
"My precious child, I love you and will never leave you.
Never, ever, during your trials and testings.
When you saw only one set of footprints,
It was then that I carried you."

God's view may be one that we don't fully understand until the other side of Glory.

It is one when looked down upon, seems clear to an eternal eye.

As much as His ways are higher and different from ours, it sure is worth trying to navigate along the way.

Many times the story of Job replays in my mind.

One of give. Take away. Give back. Blessing. Cursing.

And I often think how thankful I am that I live on this side of Job's life and example.

Realizing that God sees the bigger picture of our lives and what will bring Him the glory, is what matters.

So when I look back on my own life and only see the one set of footprints.

I really was never alone.

Even when caught in the deepest pit, He bent down and snatched me up from the rocks of despair, showing me the road once again.

As much as God will accomplish His purpose for our lives, I believe there is a part we must play.

We need to be watchful.

Watchful for His loving kindness.

Watchful for His tenderness. His care.

So when He reaches down from heaven with His finger, He is able to touch the depths of your soul. He is able to break through all the hurts.

All your preconceived ideas.

All your dreams.

Your responsibility will be to look up, seek the things above, and hold on for the ride of your life.

He will give you glimpses of His ways as you gaze on the Giver of Life.

My desire is to accept God's plans for my life even when I don't fully understand the way He goes about the drive to the destination.

I want to love God with all of my heart.

Obey His ways.

Teach His statutes.

Trust Him with the outcome.

And when I doubt that He knows best, I need to remind myself of truths from His Word.

He will keep me as the apple of His eye.
See Psalm 17:8

He delights in my way.
See Psalm 37:23

He guards me with His angels.
See Psalm 91:11

He will work out His plan for my life.
See Psalm 138:8

His thoughts of me outnumber the grains of sand.
See Psalm 139:18

He has redeemed and forgiven my sins.
See Colossians 1:14

He has made me complete.
See Colossians 2:10

God's view may be one of completion.

But it is about the journey as well as the destination.

The journey to a satisfied life.

The journey to accepting your lot in life.

The journey with much or little.

What might be the view of those who watch you travel your journey?

At times it may be just like Jesus with His few friends, Peter, James, and John in Gethsemane before he was handed over to the soldiers by Judas.

This is the event where Jesus told the apostles to stand by to . . .

Watch.

Pray.

He went a little beyond them to be with His Father. What happened upon Jesus' return?

Jesus found them asleep three different times.
See Matthew 26: 36-50

There are times we are going to have to allow our friends to stand by to watch and pray.

To stand by while we go deeper still with our heavenly Father.

You may be at a point where you need to free up your friends from the place where only God should be.

At the forefront of your life.

And that "little beyond" will be where God will bring clarity to the unknown road ahead.

It will be where He touches you in spiritual and emotional places you never imagined.

It will be where you begin to understand His will in all of what may seem confusing.

It is the place where only you and God can meet and no one can go there with you.

The connection will be a sweet time of intimacy with your Abba Father.

What I promise you, from this time alone, from this "little beyond" moment, is that you will come out of the encounter different from when you went in.

It is to be hoped that you will begin to accept the road that lies ahead of you.

As I think of my biggest supporter, John, there are times I wish I knew what he was thinking.

Even though we journeyed together and talked openly about our fears.

Our joys.

Our future.

One just can't fully grasp the emotions felt by the other.

I remember the night before one of my surgeries, we were in a hotel room.

After our goodnight kiss, he and I turned our separate ways.

It was then that I realized it was just me and God.

No matter how much John loved me and I enjoyed the touch of his hand, it was only God that mattered.

It was only my relationship with Him in the end that would save me.

It is so important to have your relationship right with God.

When you turn over in your bed, who do you turn to?

At the end of each day, review your day in your mind.

Reflect on the things you have done.

The things you have said.

Talk with God about all of it.

Look in the rearview mirror and make the necessary adjustments so that you will be able to walk in a manner worthy of your calling:

To act justly.

To love mercy.

To walk humbly with your God.

There were times, I asked John how he did it all?

"You do what you have to do," he said.

As a woman, I was looking for so much more than that answer.

I was looking for the deeper meaning of what lay behind the man who reared our girls.

Washed their clothes.

Changed their diapers.

Tucked them into bed at night.

Cared for all their needs.

Worked a demanding job.

Visited me daily.

Sometimes, I believe I over-think it. I complicate it.

When it is as simple as doing what you need to do with the strength God gives in the moment you have.

John is a husband and dad who lives out the vow.

To be my husband.

To have and to hold.

To be my constant friend.

To be my faithful partner.

In sickness and in health.

In good times and bad.

In joy and sorrow.

He promised to love me unconditionally.

To honor and respect me.

To laugh and to cry with me.

To cherish me as long as I shall live.

Yes, he went far above the call of duty.

A higher calling.

That when watched, became the view respected and admired by all.

"Do what you can,

with what you have, where you are."

Theodore Roosevelt

Chapter Nine

Turn Up the Music and Sing Along

Here we are at the fun part of the trip. Turn up the music and sing along.

Nothing is more fun for our family than when John pops in his music from the 70s and 80s.

We all start to sing in the car.

We have even turned up the music while in the middle of a vast lake on a boat.

Now that was fun because we were able to dance along, too (not that we haven't tried to in the car).

Our dogs even joined in on the fun, harmonizing with us in their unique way.

You are probably thinking, what a sight?

And you are right.

It is a sight to be seen. A sound to be heard.

But, usually, we don't care what others think of our silliness.

We just enjoy the time together and the wholesome fun jammin' out.

With joy!

Through the journey of my life, there have been some bumps, detours, and difficulties for sure, but they are a dim memory when compared to the joys.

The discoveries.

The strengths God has blessed me with along the way.

It is my love for Him that makes me just want to turn up the music and sing along with Him and enjoy the ride to the destination of His choice.

I am sure of one thing: Without the hazards and detours, I wouldn't be able to turn up the music as loud as I do.

When you have been healed Spiritually. Physically. Emotionally.

No one knows what God can do with a willing vessel.

It is through the heartaches that I met Jesus at a deeper place than I could have known Him otherwise.

My intimate encounters with Him allowed me to see Him in ways I never deemed possible.

Even though God has met me at every curve, He also revealed Himself on the straightaway of my life.

The ordinary day-to-day responsibilities.

During my morning quiet time.

The daily walks with my dogs.

The kitchen sink.

Yes, even the shower.

You have to watch for Him.

He shows up when you least expect it.

He shows up in the ordinary of your days, and it can be a disguise of the divine plan He has for you.

Don't look for burning bushes, swirling mists, rolling clouds. Don't look for a figure larger than life, brighter than day.

He is Life.

He is the Light.

Look for your Driver, your Guide, your Protector, your Provider.

Ordinary men and women from God's word, called by an extraordinary God:

Noah was found in his righteousness of daily living.

Abraham from his family life.

Moses pasturing his father-in-law's flock.

David tending the sheep.

Gideon threshing the wheat.

Samuel sleeping in the night.

Jeremiah in his youth.

Apostles during their day jobs.

Mary during her engagement.

Paul's travel on the road to Damascus to persecute believers of Christ.

For me, I have had a little of both—the ordinary, the not so ordinary.

Let me take you back to as far as I can remember and you determine if it is the ordinary or the extraordinary.

At a Women of Faith event in 1996 in my hometown, as I sat in the audience listening to the speakers, the words of the counselor who cared for me in the psychiatric hospital, just three years before, ran through my mind. "Someday you will be sharing this experience to a listening world."

It was at that event, I felt God call me into a teaching and speaking ministry.

I didn't share this with anyone but my mother-in-law, who attended the conference with me. Through battling Cushing's Syndrome, I knew there was more than just surviving.

That God may use my story in a way that would encourage others.

At the time it was hard to understand God's will in it all, and even when I felt God's call, I didn't know what it was going to look like.

But I trusted Him with the outcome.

Although, I felt God's call on my life in 1996, it was a twelve-year wait until I received my first invitation to share at another church.

It was just an ordinary day for me when I received an email invitation from a woman who had read an article I wrote for our denominational E-newsletter.

During the twelve-year preparation, I studied God's word feverishly through multiple Bible studies.

Started an Inter-denominational Bible study in our community.

Held a neighborhood study.

Organized a prison Bible study.

Worked with girls from a local nearby college through Fellowship of Christian Athletes.

During these commitments, I battled the seasons of my disease.

Amazed that when you are just living life, God is glorified in the ordinary events of obedience.

During these small gatherings, I was able to share what I was learning from God through the journey.

All the experiences built on one another and prepared me for the open door God called me to enter many years later.

There were times I felt discouraged that God didn't move a little faster in the process.

I wanted to hurry Him along.

But through a tough lesson, God wanted me to be willing to speak to one woman not a multitude of women.

You see, I thought my sharing would be to a sanctuary of hundreds, but what God wanted and what I thought was very different. Humbled by a song I listened to while waiting to pick up my then pre-schooler, God spoke to my heart, "Are you willing to speak to one person?"

When I finally bent the knee to His plan and was willing to speak to that one person, God began to use me and yes, it was to one woman.

Although the first attempt didn't work out the way I planned with this one woman.

Sadness overtook me as I watched her walk away from a short-lived marriage.

Some fifteen years later, she reconnected with me and shared how our time together affected her and what she learned from that experience. How she had watched God use me in the lives of more women.

What I thought would be a call to multitudes, God meant for an audience of one.

At times you wonder, *Is this what God wants from me?*

His calling on my life seemed to take longer than I anticipated.

Yet, through the waiting, I came to know God in a deeper way.

He showed me more about Himself, and I realized that the preparation time was necessary for this season of my life.

If I had stepped in front of God, it would have been a complete wreck.

I was not prepared.

You should always be learning more about Him as you journey.

As I reflected on the different people from the Bible who had to wait, I was encouraged in my own journey with God.

Be encouraged:

Noah built the ark one hundred and twenty years before the flood came.

Moses wandered in the dessert for forty years.

Jacob worked for fourteen years to win Rachel.

David became king twenty-two years after Samuel anointed him king.

Solomon spent seven years building the temple.

Joseph in captivity for fourteen years before salvation for his family.

Joshua in the wings for forty years with Moses before his leadership.

Jeremiah faithfully proclaimed God's word for forty years with no response from Judah.

Paul went away with God for training for three years before he went to the disciples.

The prophets' anticipation of the Messiah.

You and I waiting for the glorious return of Christ.

It was in the long awaited birth of Isaac to Sarah and Abraham in their old age nearing 100 years old that God's very words were proclaimed: It all happened at the time God had said it would (Genesis 21:2).

God has a plan for you.
His timing is perfect!

Remember from chapter six, Take Breaks Along the Way, that we learned how the destination is worth the wait?

One Sunday morning, I stayed home from church and as I was praying about moving forward with God, I found myself watching Dr. Charles Stanley on television.

"It is easy to obey God when we understand, but will we obey God when we don't understand?" Dr. Stanley said.

Wow, that was what I had been waiting to hear from God for over a year as I struggled for the green light to begin God's ministry through me, More of Him Ministries.

The writing process would follow closely behind.

That message by Dr. Charles Stanley and a little book, *Dream Giver,* by Bruce Wilkinson encouraged me to move out with power and strength.

I don't pretend to understand where God is taking me.

Just as you don't understand at times.

If we knew it all, we wouldn't need God, now, would we?

All things are in His timing!

I want to be found faithful where He has placed me, enjoying the ride along the way—maybe even turning up the music and singing along!

I'll never forget the summer day a dear friend invited me to a lake about an hour drive north of my home. I went to this secluded place, to prepare for the taping of my Bible study, *The Secret is Out,* a study from the book of Colossians.

It was just going to be God, me, my Bible, and my notes for two solid days.

I set the table up with all my papers.

My Bible.

My books.

And tea.

But before sitting down, I stepped out onto the patio overlooking the picturesque, glistening water with my Bible in hand and sat down to read the book of Colossians as if it were the first time I had ever read it.

As I began, I prayed to God to show up and reveal Himself in a way I would know that I was walking in His will.

What started out as an ordinary breeze turned into an extraordinary display of God's goodness. As I watched the trees in front of me blow with a slight whisper from God, I realized He was putting on a show for me.

With each praise from my lips, the trees began to rustle a little more until it seemed to be as though the trees were clapping their hands.

Every time I would be silent, the trees would slow down to a complete stop.

The more I praised and thanked God for Him and who He was, they would start up again.

It was as though I was the only one enjoying this display of beauty.

You will live in joy and peace.
The mountains and hills will burst into song,
and the trees of the field will clap their hands!

Isaiah 55:12 (NLT)

But it was just what I needed to carry on what God began in me.

You should always be learning more about God with every turn of events.

I am convinced, if you watch for Him, He will reveal Himself to those whose spiritual eyes seek Him.

And once you are aware of His presence in your life, He will build the road of opportunity to His calling on your life.

Empower you to accomplish the works He planned for you.

Reveal your beautiful purpose.

Recently, while attending a simulcast with Priscilla Shirer, she taught on Gideon's call.

What that call looked like.

Through the story of Gideon in Judges 6, I was challenged to prepare my gift for God, present it to Him, put it down on the Rock, and pour it out.

As I thought about this process and my own personal life, the preparations have been difficult at times, but Priscilla encouraged us to not despise the preparations.

I thought what a great statement.

It is in the preparation times where you meet God in ways that you never thought possible. And each preparation builds on the next until He feels you are ready to present your gift to Him. Then you must be obedient to put it down at His feet and pour it out unto Him, allowing Him to use you.

Through years of preparation and many encouraging individuals, today I am enjoying the fruit of obedience to God through full-time ministry.

And the music plays a little louder to the tune of "How Great Thou Art."

Turn up the music.

Sing along.

And even throw in a little holy jig.

Chapter Ten
Journey to a Satisfied Life

I hope through our ride together, you are enjoying your own journey with God.

You are able to look back from where He brought you.

See His handiwork all along the journey.

As He makes you into the person He wants you to become.

Looking ahead with great anticipation of what He will continue to do.

What He will continue to teach you.

And where he will continue to take you.

I believe part of my journey has been learning to be content where He has placed me.

In the potholes.

Through the detours.

Along the straightaways.

The failures.

The successes.

Learning to be content has allowed me to become satisfied with my own journey and not covet another person's journey. Not wish for someone else's ride.

I would be lying if I said there weren't times I didn't understand the road before me.

There were days of discouragement.

There were months of wonder.

There were years of expectation.

At one point in our marriage, John buying a bread company and changing careers. At the beginning of our research, I have to be honest with you, it was not where I felt God leading me. But through much face-down prayer, I realized it was where God was leading John, and I felt that I needed to support him with this endeavor. I felt a deep desire to show submission, even though I felt God's personal call on my life to something different.

With each visit to neighboring stores and a trip to the company headquarters in Montana, I could see myself enjoying the small town business.

The idea began to grow on me. Soon, I was fully engaged and ready to go.

I could see the blessing of our own business to the community, and I certainly would be able to live out my faith by serving others. Also, our girls would have a place of employment through their high school years.

The memories of "the good old days" working at my parents' business resonated within me.

It was in the acceptance of this detour over my personal plans that I learned to be satisfied where God placed me at the end of each day.

Only two weeks before breaking ground for the stand-alone store front, we realized God was closing a door to what looked open for months. And it was closing hard.

This all happened when I found out about my heart condition, which I am sure magnified the situation.

We both knew the answer! But the floor plans were drawn, the cabinets selected, the paint colors chosen and the equipment sat in our friend's barn.

God, what about my plans?

The answer: we could not move forward if God was stopping it, no matter the loss.

As the years passed from that time, we have seen God's hand upon our decision.

I knew part of it for me was to learn to be satisfied where God placed me.

To be obedient to the submission of God and the following of my husband's lead.

To embrace the testing from God and to trust Him enough to follow.

Were these months all for nothing?

Absolutely not. God used it all to prepare me for the next testing time, and the next corner we would need to skid around.

During this time, we made a visit to Florida with the girls.

Partly a visit with my parents who lived there.

Partly a Disney craze.

We rented a red convertible.

Squished our luggage in the trunk, the backseat, and under our feet.

Wherever it would fit. Oh, but we looked cool.

And felt on top of the world.

Elated with our journey, a wave of sadness crept into my mind.

Almost depression.

Where did this come from?

I did not know.

Looking out the window of the car. Gazing into the beautiful blue skies, I spoke with God. "I should be happier than anyone I know, God. Look at all you have brought me through. How can I not be grateful?"

Just then, I felt God speak to my heart.

I needed to be thankful for His Son, Jesus Christ.

Thankful for the cross.

Period.

That is what life is all about.

It's not about the acquisitions.

Accomplishments.

Activity.

Life Is Christ!

Period.

He should be the focus of our ambitions.

The reason for existence.

I don't want to be caught like the church at Ephesus in Revelation, chapter two.

Praised for my good deeds, toil, perseverance, and knowledge of false teachers.

While being admonished for walking away from my first love of God. My zeal for Jesus Christ.

I don't want to be found too busy doing God's work, but with wrong motives.

I want to always keep my relationship with God intimate.

One that heeds His call.

Have you ever wished for someone else's life?

Especially when you wait for what seems like an eternity for the one you long for?

I used to.

No one person's life, in particular.

Just different from the way it was panning out. Different from the road I was already on.

But what I realized is the road before me is just the ride God wants for me.

It is when you can accept it.

Embrace it.

Then you can enjoy the journey set before you.

When you look to God through the heartaches, He will make you radiant with joy.

> "LORD, make me to know my end
> And what is the extent of my days;
> Let me know how transient I am.
> Behold, You have made my days *as* handbreadths,
> And my lifetime as nothing in Your sight;
> Surely every man at his best is a mere breath. Selah.
> Surely every man walks about as a phantom;
> Surely they make an uproar for nothing;
> He amasses *riches* and does not know who will gather them.
> And now, Lord, for what do I wait?
> My hope is in You."
>
> Psalm 39:4-7 (NASB)

Teach us to number our days, Oh God!

That I may present to you a heart of wisdom

Psalm 90:12 (NASB)

It is not so much the days we have, but it is what we do with the days we are given.

Some have more than others. Some less.

Yesterday is gone. Tomorrow is uncertain.

Today is here—may I use it wisely!

Choose to live as though this was your last breath.

Love more deeply.

Forgive more promptly.

Give more generously.

Speak more graciously.

Care more thoughtfully.

I want to remember this when my days speed by with little thought of my effect on others.

Through the many days I have sat at the side of my dear ninety-nine year old friend, Dora, I have learned much. As far back as Sarah's preschool days, I began to gain wisdom as she spoke truth into my life.

I would pick Sarah up from her morning out and head to Dora's and Karl's for our monthly lunch date, where we would sit and listen to stories of old.

As Sarah entered elementary school, I still wouldn't miss our time around the table with Dora and Karl.

This is something that I looked forward to often.

It wasn't the accomplishments that impress me or the recipes we exchanged, although those were good too.

It was her love for her husband, her family, her grandchildren, and her great-grandchildren.

It was her endurance through illness when I wasn't sure she would make it.

It was her trust in God to complete, with grace, what He began in her life.

It was the joy in her smile.

It was the twinkle in her eyes when she would reminisce about her courting years.

It was the kindness she would speak into her listeners' ears.

It was the preparations from their garden she would prepare for the winter months ahead.

It was her desire to do good.

Her respect for her parents as she matured.

Her love for God's word.

In the end, it is what we do with Jesus that matters.

This is what I saw in Dora.

Satisfaction.

Acceptance.

Love.

But godliness with contentment is great gain.

1 Timothy 6:6 (NIV)

This is an ongoing process.

This is a deliberate approach to building relationships.

Relationships with God.

Relationships with others.

Whatever you do in word or deed,

do all in the name of the Lord Jesus,

giving thanks through him to God the Father.

Colossians 3:17 (NASB)

In the end, how you love will matter.

As I look back over this twenty-year journey with Cushings and all I have learned.

I see Him around every turn.

Every detour.

Every pit-stop

Every encounter.

Every relationship.

It may not have been clear some of the days, but His hand was perpetually upon me.

And I know I can trust Him with the days ahead.

I wait with great anticipation for the things to come.

He has taken me to the highest mountain as we climbed it together.

Walked with me through the deepest Valley.

Brought me through blazing fires.

Brushed me with colors of life.

And washed me white as snow.

Why wouldn't I trust Him with the next step I take?

The next curve I will drive around?

Won't you trust Him, too?

The Light that I received with each step along the way is what carried me when I felt like I couldn't go on.

And it is what will continue to brighten my days ahead.

Remaining in His Word is the beam of light at the end of the long dark road.

God's Word from Psalm 119 brings much to our lives.

It brings Happiness.

Purity.

Wisdom.

Revival.

Encouragement.

Life.

Freedom.

Comfort.

Good judgment.

Knowledge.

Hope.

Peace.

Light.

Guidance.

My prayer for you is that you would embrace the road before you as you make the needed adjustments from the rear view mirror.

Accept the detours along the way as stepping stones to the final destination.

Take breaks as needed.

Capture the memories.

Enjoy those who travel with you.

And most definitely turn up the music and sing along.

It's your road trip and no one else's.

Express gratitude.

Accept it.

Live it.

Love the journey.

Small Group Discussion Questions

Chapter One
It's Been a Road Trip

Go Deeper

Proverbs 16:1, 9 (ESV)

The plans of the heart belong to man,
but the answer of the tongue is from the LORD.
The heart of man plans his way,
But the LORD directs his steps.

Philippians 3:8 (NASB)

More than that, I count all things to be loss in view of
the surpassing value of knowing Christ Jesus my Lord, for
whom I have suffered the loss of all things, and count them
but rubbish so that I may gain Christ.

Questions for Reflection and Discussion

During a Bible study by Beth Moore, I read: "There are three different scenarios when people of God face fiery trials: we can be delivered from, delivered through, and delivered by. The first scenario, delivered from, will build our faith, the second scenario, of being delivered through, will refine our faith and the last, we will be delivered by the fire into our heavenly Father's arms, which will perfect our faith."[1]

As I look back on the years the Lord has given me, I am thankful He has delivered me through the fire and for the years of refining my character.

What about you?

1. What is God delivering you through? Share your road trip with your group.

2. How well do you adjust to God's plans?

3. Is your journey leading you into the destination of Jesus' loving arms?

---

1. Beth Moore, Daniel, Lives of Integrity; Words of Prophesy (Nashville, TN: LifeWay Press, 2006), 46.

Chapter Two
God, What About My Plans?

Go Deeper

Jeremiah 29:11 (NASB)

"For I know the plans that I have for you,"
declares the Lord,
"plans for welfare and not for calamity
to give you a future and a hope."

Psalm 147:10-11 (NASB)

He does not delight in the strength of the horse;
He does not take pleasure in the legs of a man.
The LORD favors those who fear Him,
Those who wait for His lovingkindness.

Ecclesiastes 7:13-14 (NIV)

Consider what God has done:
Who can straighten what he has made crooked?
When times are good, be happy;
but when times are bad, consider this:
God has made the one as well as the other.
Therefore, no one can discover
anything about their future.

Questions for Reflection and Discussion

1. Are your plans God's plans?

2. How is God drawing you onto Himself in this season of your life? Are you using His strength or your own strength?

3. Are you able to look at your situation a little different after reading this chapter?

Chapter Three

Rearview Mirror

Go Deeper

Deuteronomy 6:4-9 (NIV)

Hear, O Israel:
The LORD our God, the LORD is one.
Love the LORD your God with all your heart
and with all your soul and with all your strength.
These commandments that I give you today
are to be on your hearts.
Impress them on your children.
Talk about them when you sit at home
and when you walk along the road,
when you lie down and when you get up.
Tie them as symbols on your hands
and bind them on your foreheads.
Write them on the doorframes of your houses
and on your gates.

Ephesians 4:1-6 (NIV)

As a prisoner for the Lord, then,
I urge you to live a life
worthy of the calling you have received.
Be completely humble and gentle;
be patient, bearing with one another in love.
Make every effort to keep the unity of the Spirit
through the bond of peace.
There is one body and one Spirit,
just as you were called to one hope
when you were called;
one Lord, one faith, one baptism;
one God and Father of all,
who is over all and through all and in all.

Questions for Reflection and Discussion

1. Reflect on days that are behind you and the impact they have made on the person you have become.

2. What are you doing to pass down the love of God to your children and grandchildren?

3. There are adjustments that you are able to make because of choices. What do you need to adjust to walk in a manner worthy of the Lord?

Chapter Four

There's a Traffic Jam

Go Deeper

Psalm 68:35 (NASB)

O God, *You are* awesome from Your sanctuary.
The God of Israel Himself
gives strength and power to the people.
Blessed be God!

1 Peter 1:7 (NLT)

These trials will show that your faith is genuine.
It is being tested
as fire tests and purifies gold
though your faith is far more precious than mere gold.
So when your faith remains strong through many trials,
it will bring you much praise and glory and honor
on the day when Jesus Christ
is revealed to the whole world.

Questions for Reflection and Discussion

1. What are some of the lessons you have learned in the traffic jams of your life?

2. Which of the benefits listed in the traffic jams, have been valuable to you?

3. When others watch your reactions to the traffic jams of your life, what do they see?

Chapter Five
Enjoy Your Fellow Travelers

Go Deeper

Proverbs 17:17 (NIV)

A friend loves at all times,
And a brother is born for adversity.

1 Thessalonians 4:9-10 (NLT)

But we don't need to write to you
about the importance of loving each other,
for God himself has taught you to love one another.
Indeed, you already show your love
for all the believers throughout Macedonia.
Even so, dear brothers and sisters,
we urge you to love them even more.

Questions for Reflection and Discussion

1. Share with your group, some of the traits of your good friends that you would like to emulate.

2. What is the hardest part of humbling yourself? Why?

3. Is God placing on your heart a particular area He wants you to excel your love for Him to the next level?

Chapter Six

Take Breaks Along the Way

Go Deeper

Deuteronomy 30:19-20 (NASB)

"I call heaven and earth to witness against you today,
that I have set before you life and death,
the blessing and the curse.
So choose life in order that you may live,
you and your descendants,
by loving the LORD your God,
by obeying His voice,
and by holding fast to Him;
for this is your life and the length of your days,
that you may live in the land
which the LORD swore to your fathers,
to Abraham, Isaac, and Jacob, to give them."

John 14:27 (NLT)

"I am leaving you with a gift—
peace of mind and heart.
And the peace I give
is a gift the world cannot give.
So don't be troubled or afraid."

Questions for Reflection and Discussion

1. Share a time when God asked you to take a break and wait on Him.

2. What was the outcome?

3. What did you learn?

4. What are you "holding onto God" for at this time? How does it make you feel to think that God longs to spend time with you? What do you need to eliminate or change to have a richer "sanctuary" time with Him?

Chapter Seven

Capture the Memories

Go Deeper

Isaiah 55:8-9 (NIV)

"For my thoughts are not your thoughts,
neither are your ways my ways," declares the LORD.
"As the heavens are higher than the earth,
so are my ways higher than your ways
and my thoughts than your thoughts."

Philippians 4:14 (NASB)

Nevertheless, you have done well
to share *with me* in my affliction.

Questions for Reflection and Discussion

1. Share a memory captured that changed the
    course of your direction?

2. What are some of the teachable moments you
    have learned in the darkness?

3. Write the snapshots taken that, at first glance,
    seemed to be a bump in the road but became a
    blessing upon further review.

Chapter Eight

One Road, Two Views

Go Deeper

2 Corinthians 4:17 (NIV)

For our light and momentary troubles
are achieving for us an eternal glory
that far outweighs them all.

Psalm 25:15 (NASB)

My eyes are continually toward the LORD,
For He will pluck my feet out of the net.

Jessie Seneca

Questions for Reflection and Discussion

1. Remember, your responsibility is to look up, seek the things above, and hold on for the ride of your life. What is God asking you to look up for during this season of your life?

2. Who are the friends you need to release from your expectations of satisfying your needs?

3. Have you gone to that "little beyond" place with God? What is He teaching you?

Chapter Nine

Turn Up the Music and Sing Along

Go Deeper

Ephesians 2:10 (NASB)

For we are His workmanship,
created in Christ Jesus for good works,
which God prepared beforehand
so that we would walk in them.

2 Chronicles 16:9a (NASB)

For the eyes of the LORD move to and fro
throughout the earth
that He may strongly support those
whose heart is completely His.

Questions for Reflection and Discussion

1. Share a fun story of when you turned up the music and sang along.

2. When has God shown up to you in an extraordinary way through an ordinary activity?

3. What closed door are you still waiting for God to open? Are you finding it hard to enjoy the preparation?

Chapter Ten

Journey to a Satisfied Life

Go Deeper

Hebrews 3:13 (NIV)

But encourage one another daily,
as long as it is called "Today,"
so that none of
you may be hardened by sin's deceitfulness.

Phillipians 3:8 (NLT)

Yes, everything else is worthless
when compared with the infinite value
of knowing Christ Jesus my Lord.
For his sake I have discarded everything else,
counting it all as garbage, so that I could gain Christ.

Questions for Reflection and Discussion

1. What have you learned about your own journey through Jessie's story?

2. What is God speaking into your heart?

3. Is there something you need to change in your day to make your days more productive and to guard your margin time?

About the Author

Jessie Seneca is a national speaker, author, leadership trainer, and the founder of More of Him Ministries. She has a passion to help women experience God's Word for themselves as she encourages them to move into a life fully devoted to God.

Jessie and her husband, John, live in Bethlehem, Pennsylvania, and have two young adult daughters.

Visit Jessie at www.MoreofHimMinistries.org.

Did you know that God has a secret? One day, while Jessie Seneca was reading Colossians 1:27 in the New Living Translation (NLT), she saw it. There it was, God's secret: "Christ lives in you. This gives you assurance of sharing in His glory." Once you know it, you will never be the same. You can enter into a wholehearted relationship with the supreme and all-sufficient Christ. This study features five weeks of personal, daily assignments and six weekly group sessions with DVD (available separately). As this study guides you into a deeper relationship with your heavenly Father and Savior, Jesus Christ, you will be grounded in the truth of Christ, the person of Christ, and the power of Christ. You will be challenged in your everyday relationships—in the home, workplace, and church. Read and study the short yet compelling and powerful letter of Colossians. When you are finished studying it, you will not only want to learn the secret for yourself, but live it out and pass it on.

A companion DVD and audio CD are available for this title.

Order Info.

For autographed books, bulk order discounts,
or to schedule speaking engagements, contact
Jessie Seneca
jessie@jessieseneca.com
610.216.2730

Like us on Facebook!

To order Jessie's books
visit www.MoreofHimMinistries.org

Also available from your favorite bookstore

Fruitbearer Publilshing, LLC
302.856.6649 • FAX 302.856.7742
info@fruitbearer.com
www.fruitbearer.com
P.O. Box 777, Georgetown, DE 19947

Made in the USA
Charleston, SC
09 November 2013